What's in this book

学习内容 Contents   2

读一读 Read   4

听听说说 Listen and say   12

写一写 Write   16

多元学习 Connections   18

温习 Checkpoint   20

分享 Sharing   22

This book belongs to

T0351536

_____

花与果 Flowers and fruit

学习内容 Contents

沟通 Communication

说说花和果实
Talk about flowers and fruit

生词 New words

⭐ 甜	sweet
⭐ 草莓	strawberry
⭐ 梨	pear
⭐ 得	(used between a verb and its complement to indicate the degree)
⭐ 桃子	peach
⭐ 香蕉	banana
⭐ 有意思	interesting
⭐ 看见	to see
⭐ 盘	(measure word for dishes)
跟	and
粉红色	pink
棕色	brown

背景介绍：
图片中的是草莓、香蕉、梨和桃子以及它们的花。

句式 Sentence patterns

梨比草莓大得多。
A pear is much bigger than a strawberry.

花开得美。
Flowers are so beautiful.

跨学科学习 Project

种植草莓，并用图表记录
它的生长
Grow some strawberries and
record their growth

参考答案：
1 My favourite fruits are strawberries/
   watermelons/grapes.
2 Yes, I have./Maybe, but I did not pay attention
   to it.
3 Yes, they are strawberry, banana, pear and
   peach./I know the fruit but do not know their
   flowers.

文化 Cultures

和水果相关的中文和英文成语
Chinese and English idioms related
to fruit

Get ready

1 What is your favourite fruit?

2 Have you ever seen the flowers of that fruit?

3 Do you know the flowers and fruit in the picture?

读一读 Read

故事大意：
介绍水果和它们的花，认识大自然的美。

tián
甜

草莓红红的部分是假果，是花托在传播花粉后变大的部分，真正的草莓果实反倒是布满草莓表面的众多小点。

参考问题和答案：

1 Which fruit do these flowers produce? How can you tell? (The strawberry. Because the leaves are the same.)

2 What can you say about the taste of strawberries and cherries? (They are sweet.)

你知道这是什么水果的花吗？这种水果红红的，很甜。

lí
梨

de
得

gēn
跟

cǎo méi
草莓

用在动词或形容词后的连接补语，表示效果或程度。
如：跑～快。甜～多。

参考问题和答案：

1 Do you like strawberries and pears? (Yes, I do./ I like strawberries only.)

2 Is the pear much bigger than the strawberry? (Yes, it is much bigger.)

3 Do you think that the strawberry flower and the pear flower look alike? (Yes, they do.)

这是草莓。草莓的花跟梨的花有点儿像，但是梨比草莓大得多。

桃子原产于中国，最远
可以追溯到周朝，约前
11世纪——前256年。

桃花为淡至深粉红或红色，有时为白色。

tāo zi
桃子

zōng sè
棕色

fěn hóng sè
粉红色

桃子长在棕色的树枝上，它的花是粉红色或者白色的。

参考问题和答案：

1 What fruit is the girl holding? (She is holding a peach.)

2 Peaches grow on the branches of a peach tree. What colour is the tree branch? (It is brown.)

3 Do you like the pink peach flowers? (Yes, I do./They are OK.)

yǒu yì si
有意思

香蕉花是香蕉树的花
蕾，香蕉树一生只有
一个香蕉花花蕾。

xiāng jiāo
香蕉

香蕉的花很有意思，它又大又红，
跟香蕉不像。

参考问题和答案：

1 What fruit is the girl holding? (She is holding some bananas.)

2 The banana flower is big. Do you think it is interesting? (Yes, it looks funny/strange.)

3 How often do you eat bananas? (Every day./Once a week./Not often.)

苹果

柠檬

橙

黑莓

大自然真奇妙！花开得美，不同的花结出不同的果实。

参考问题和答案：

1　What fruits are shown in the pictures? (They are apples, lemons, oranges and berries.)

2　Do these fruits grow from the same flowers? (No, they grow from different flowers.)

苹果

葡萄

梨

葡萄

李子

李子花

kàn jiàn
看见

pán
盘

量词，用于表示数量。
如：一盘水果。

当你看见这盘水果时，想过它们
生长的故事吗？

参考问题和答案：

1 What can the children see in front of them? (They can see a plate of fruit.)

2 What do you think the children are thinking about? (They are thinking about how different fruits grow from different flowers.)

Let's think

1 Recall the story. Match the fruits to their flowers.

2 Make an interesting breakfast and describe it. Paste your photo below.

这只狮子真有意思！它的眼睛是葡萄，鼻子是桃子，脸上还有草莓。我喜欢这只水果狮子！你做的是什么呢？

提醒学生先洗干净水果和手才开始做早餐，同时不要浪费食物。

Paste your photo here.

这是我做的……

New words

延伸活动：
让学生尽量用生词看图说话。参考表述：艾文跟
爱莎在餐馆里看见很多水果：有红色的草莓、苹果
跟荔枝；有黄色的梨跟香蕉；有绿色的葡萄；还有
粉红色的桃子。他们还看见一个有意思的"人"。

 1 Learn the new words.

看见　盘　桃子　粉红色　草莓　甜　香蕉　有意思　棕色　梨　得　跟

2 Listen to your teacher and point to the correct words above.

听听说说 Listen and say

 1 Listen and circle the correct letters.

1 水果蛋糕里没有哪个水果？

   a 草莓

   b 香蕉

   ⓒ 梨

2 爸爸买了什么颜色的花？

   a 粉红色

   b 粉红色或红色

   ⓒ 粉红色和红色

3 他们跟妈妈说了有水果蛋糕和花吗？

   a 说了

   ⓑ 没说

   c 正在说

4 他们为什么做蛋糕？为什么买花？

   ⓐ 因为今天是妈妈的生日。

   b 因为今天休息。

   c 因为今天天气好。

2 Look at the pictures. Listen to the story c

①

 这些是我新买的水果，很甜。

 今天的草莓比前天的大得多。

③

 你怎么不吃？

 我想等到晚上吃。

 为什么？

第一题录音稿：
今天是妈妈的生日。我和弟弟做了一个水果蛋糕，里面有草莓、香蕉和桃子。都是妈妈喜欢吃的水果。爸爸买了粉红色和红色的花，花开得很漂亮。但是我们没有跟妈妈说，她看见了会笑得很快乐。

这里还有梨和葡萄。

这些都是我喜欢的水果。

我想等爸爸和弟弟回来再吃，大家一起吃比一个人吃高兴得多。

第二题参考问题和答案：
1 What fruits can you see in the story? (Apples, strawberries, bananas, oranges, grapes and pears.)
2 Which of them is your favourite? (Strawberries/oranges/pears.)

3 Write the letters and say.

a 得　b 跟　c 有意思　d 看见

1

爸爸 _b_ 爷爷的样子有点儿像，但爸爸比爷爷高 _a_ 多。

2

我 _d_ 长颈鹿和斑马在喝水。

3
我喜欢带小狗去海边玩，我觉得很 _c_。

Task

Paste the photos of the flowers of the apple and grapes below. Talk about the fruit with your friend.

这是苹果，它生长在……它的花……

草莓生长在地上。先开出白色的花，花开得很漂亮，然后长出红色的草莓。草莓不大，但是很甜。

Paste your photo here.

Paste your photo here.

这是葡萄跟葡萄的花……

Game

告诉学生玩游戏时如碰到不会说的食物名称，可以上网搜寻以培养自发学习精神。

Follow the two food paths and find out what they lead to. Colour the food as you go along. Talk about the pictures and say the names of the food with your friend.

你有健康的牙齿。你笑得真漂亮！

我用/不用去看牙医，因为我画了……然后画了……我喜欢吃……跟……

你要去看牙医！

Chant

老师准备歌词中各水果的花的照片，并让学生带真实水果回学校，说唱至某一水果时，学生用手分别指向该水果及其相应的花。

🎧 **Listen and say.**

香蕉长，桃子圆，
草莓小，梨子大。

香蕉的花是红色的，
桃子的花是粉红色的，
草莓的花是白色的，
梨的花也是白色的。

花开得多，开得好，
水果长得大，长得好。

参考用法见下：

生活用语 Daily expressions

有意思。
It's interesting.

这本书很好看，有意思。

没意思。
It's boring.

这个游戏不好玩，没意思。

写一写 Write

1 Trace and write the characters.

提醒学生"得"为左右结构；"有"和"思"
为上下结构；"意"为上中下结构。

丿 ノ 彳 彳 彳 彳 彳 彳 彳 得 得 得

得	得		

一 ナ 才 有 有 有

丶 亠 亠 立 产 音 音 音 音 意 意 意

丶 口 曰 田 田 思 思 思

有	意	思	有	意	思

2 Write and say.

这是我最喜欢
吃的糖果，它
是粉红色的，
比草莓甜<u>得</u>多。

真 <u>有意思</u>！
我还想再玩儿
一次。

延伸活动：
填好空后，学生仔细读一次段落加深理解。然后两人一组，在不看段落的情况下，
尝试用第三者的身份说说该段落的内容。

3 Fill in the blanks with the correct words. Colour the horses using the same colours.

昨天，爸爸妈妈带我去看跑马。我 <u>看见</u> 很多马，
棕色跟黑色的都有，它们都很漂亮。

跑马开始后，马都跑 <u>得</u> 很快。我 <u>看见</u> 骑马的人
<u>站</u> 着， <u>站</u> <u>得</u> 很高。跑马真 <u>有意思</u> ！

拼音输入法 Pinyin input

Fill in the blanks. Number the sentences to make a meaningful paragraph. Type the paragraph and read it to your friend.

1 我会中文，我已经学了<u>三</u>年。

3 但是中文很有<u>意</u>思，我喜欢学。

2 开始学<u>中</u>文时，我觉得它很难。

5 我也能打更多汉字。我真喜欢中文！

4 现在，我能写很多汉字，还写<u>得</u>很好。

告诉学生应先找段落中心句（"我会中文，……"）；然后找具体描述中心句的内容（"开始学……"
和"但是中文……"），并从关键词"但是"得出该句应放在后面；然后找与"开始学……"相对的
"现在，我……"最后找段落总结句（"我真喜欢中文！"）。

多元学习 Connections

告诉学生汉语成语的形式以四字格居多，一般不能任意变动词序，抽换或增减其中的成分。学完以下成语后，可尝试用其简单描述某同学和某老师。如：他孔融让梨，给哥哥吃大的苹果，自己吃小的。/王老师有很多学生，桃李满门。

1 Learn about two Chinese idioms that are related to fruit.

> 我们应该学会孔融让梨。

In ancient China, Kong Rong, a four-year-old boy, gave the larger pears to his brothers and saved the smaller one for himself. His act exemplified the value of courtesy and humility that a child should have and hence the idiom 孔融让梨 (kǒng róng ràng lí).

> 我长大了，也想做一个好老师，可以桃李满门。

桃李满门 (táo lǐ mǎn mén) refers to a respected teacher having lots of good students all around the world.

2 Some English idioms are also about fruit. Write the correct letters.

> a 苹果 b 有用 c 没用 d 生气 e 香蕉

compare apples and oranges
比一比___a___和橙子 (orange)，
这是___c___的。

go bananas
___d___

问问学生有没有种盆栽或水果的经验，让有经验的学生与大家分享他们的心得。
然后告诉学生植物生长的必要因素：阳光、空气和水。为图片排序后，考考学生
草莓红色、大大的部分到底是不是水果，答案见本教师书第4页注解。

1 Do you know how to grow strawberries? Research and number the pictures.

浇水 [2]

开花 [3]

sunlight

air

从土中长出来 [1]

结水果 [4]

草莓的生长，要有阳光
(sunlight)、空气 (air)
和水。

2 It's your turn now. Grow some strawberries and record their growth.
Then report to your classmates.

a 晴天　b 刮风　c 下雨　d 下雪　e 多云

日期	___月___日	___月___日	___月___日	___月___日
天气				
高度	___ cm	___ cm	___ cm	___ cm
颜色	__色	__色	__色	__色
样子				

……月……日，草莓长出来了！长得很红、很多。

提醒学生常年草莓是最流行的草莓，可在花圃或容器中生长，户外适宜温带气候条件，室内则宜放置在寒冷的地方。

1 Know more about yourself. Complete the questionnaire. Read the questions and tick the boxes. Then calculate your score.

		a never	b sometimes	c oft
1	你吃饭前会洗手吗？	☐	☐	☐
2	你吃水果吃得多吗？	☐	☐	☐
3	你吃蔬菜吃得多吗？	☐	☐	☐
4	你吃甜的食物吃得多吗？	☐	☐	☐
5	你晚上会睡十个小时吗？	☐	☐	☐
6	你看电视看得多吗？	☐	☐	☐
7	你玩电脑玩得多吗？	☐	☐	☐
8	你做运动做得多吗？	☐	☐	☐
9	你骑自行车骑得多吗？	☐	☐	☐
10	你会走路上学吗？	☐	☐	☐

计分表

1	a1	b2	c3	d4	**6**	a4	b3	c2	d1
2	a1	b2	c3	d4	**7**	a4	b3	c2	d1
3	a1	b2	c3	d4	**8**	a1	b2	c3	d4
4	a4	b3	c2	d1	**9**	a1	b2	c3	d4
5	a1	b2	c3	d4	**10**	a1	b2	c3	d4

分析

32-40 你真健康！

23-31 你有一点儿不健康。

14-22 你不太健康。

我有……分。我很喜欢吃水果，草莓、香蕉、桃子跟梨，我都喜欢吃。我有时候会玩飞盘，但是我很少运动。所以我有一点儿不健康。你呢？

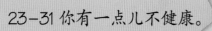

评核方法：
学生两人一组，互相考察评价表内单词和句子的听说读写。交际沟通部分由老师朗读要求，学生再互相对话。如果达到了某项技能要求，则用色笔将星星或小辣椒涂色。

d always

☐
☐
☐
☐
☐
☐
☐
☐
☐
☐

看见分数了吗？
你有多少分？

我有……分。
我的……

2 Work with your friend. Colour the stars and the chillies.

Words and sentences	说	读	写
甜	☆	☆	🌶
草莓	☆	☆	🌶
梨	☆	☆	🌶
得	☆	☆	☆
桃子	☆	☆	🌶
香蕉	☆	☆	🌶
有意思	☆	☆	☆
看见	☆	☆	🌶
盘	☆	☆	🌶
跟	☆	🌶	🌶
粉红色	☆	🌶	🌶
棕色	☆	🌶	🌶
梨比草莓大得多。	☆	🌶	🌶
花开得美。	☆	🌶	🌶

Talk about flowers and fruit	☆

3 What does your teacher say?

评核建议：
根据学生课堂表现，分别给予"太棒了！(Excellent!)"、"不错！(Good!)"或"继续努力！(Work harder!)"的评价，再让学生圈出左侧对应的表情，以记录自己的学习情况。

21

Words I remember

甜	tián	sweet
草莓	cǎo méi	strawberry
梨	lí	pear
得	de	(used between a verb and its complement to indicate the degree)
桃子	táo zi	peach
香蕉	xiāng jiāo	banana
有意思	yǒu yì si	interesting
看见	kàn jiàn	to see
盘	pán	(measure word for dishes)
跟	gēn	and
粉红色	fěn hóng sè	pink
棕色	zōng sè	brown

延伸活动：
1 学生用手遮盖英文，读中文单词，并思考单词意思；
2 学生用手遮盖中文单词，看着英文说出对应的中文单词；
3 学生两人一组，尽量运用中文单词分角色复述第4至9页内容。

Other words

果实	guǒ shí	fruit
长	zhǎng	to grow
树枝	shù zhī	branch
奇妙	qí miào	amazing
开	kāi	to open out
结	jié	to form
出	chū	to put forth
当	dāng	when
过	guò	(auxiliary word of tense)
生长	shēng zhǎng	to grow
故事	gù shi	story
孔融让梨	kǒng róng ràng lí	(to show the value of courtesy and humility)
桃李满门	táo lǐ mǎn mén	(a respected teacher with lots of good students)
橙子	chéng zi	orange
阳光	yáng guāng	sunlight
空气	kōng qì	air

OXFORD
UNIVERSITY PRESS

Oxford University Press is a department of the University of Oxford.
It furthers the University's objective of excellence in research, scholarship,
and education by publishing worldwide. Oxford is a registered trade mark of
Oxford University Press in the UK and in certain other countries

Published in Hong Kong by
Oxford University Press (China) Limited
39th Floor, One Kowloon, 1 Wang Yuen Street, Kowloon Bay,
Hong Kong

© Oxford University Press (China) Limited 2017

The moral rights of the author have been asserted

First Edition published in 2017

All rights reserved. No part of this publication may be reproduced, stored in a
retrieval system, or transmitted, in any form or by any means, without the prior
permission in writing of Oxford University Press (China) Limited, or as expressly
permitted by law, by licence, or under terms agreed with the appropriate
reprographics rights organization. Enquiries concerning reproduction outside
the scope of the above should be sent to the Rights Department, Oxford
University Press (China) Limited, at the address above

You must not circulate this work in any other form
and you must impose this same condition on any acquirer

Illustrated by Anne Lee, Emily Chan and Wildman

Photographs for reproduction permitted by Dreamstime.com

China National Publications Import & Export (Group) Corporation is an authorized distributor of
Oxford Elementary Chinese.

Please contact content@cnpiec.com.cn or 86-10-65856782

ISBN: 978-0-19-082314-6

10 9 8 7 6 5 4 3 2

Teacher's Edition
ISBN: 978-0-19-082326-9

10 9 8 7 6 5 4 3 2